I0558996

Books Academy LLC
112 SW H K Dodgen Loop Temple, Texas 76504
Hotline: (254) 800-1189

Ordering Information:

Quantity sales. Special discounts are available on quantity purchases by corporations, associations, and others. For details, contact the publisher at the address above.

Printed in the United States of America.

ISBN-13: Paperback: 978-1-968807-14-6
           eBook: 978-1-968807-15-3

Library of Congress Control Number: 2025917296

I am writing this to be an encouragement to others. I pray this will be a help to some that may be struggling with things in their life. I have made many mistakes and wasted a lot of time for God over the 45 plus years that I have been saved, and I am praying that others will be able to see how the Lord has worked in my life. Maybe others will be able to do more for God than I did from reading this. Just keep trusting in the Lord and see what He can do for you and with you.

What Happens When We Put Our Faith and Trust in God

One night, when I could not sleep, I looked at the stars out my window, and a thought came to my mind. God has created all the stars, and not one of them is the same. Just as all the stars are different, so is every one of us. God has created all of us to be different, whether in size, color, language, even where we live. There is a purpose for everyone. We must decide what we are going to do with our lives. The best thing we can do is serve the Lord, do what He wants, and be where He wants us to be.

> *"But seek ye first the kingdom of*
> *God, and his righteousness; and*
> *all these things shall be added*
> *unto you." - Matthew 6:33*

God has been so good to me; I could never repay the Lord for what He has done in my life. Time and time again, the Lord has always been there for me. It does not matter where I am or when it is; He is always there. God is always good and right. We do not always know why things happen in our lives, but God has a reason and a purpose. We often take things for granted, like what we have, and we only think about ourselves. If we look at the big picture of the world and see how many people live in poverty and without God, we will realize how good we have it in America.

Our America was started on God's Word with many faithful men. America has fallen so far away from what path she started on. God is still in the same place He was when America started. Christians have not been doing their part for many years, including me. Churches have fallen away from the standards of what God wants us to be doing. I do not know whether God will bless America again before He comes back.

"If my people, which are called by my name, shall humble themselves, and pray, and seek my face, and turn from their wicked ways; then will I hear from heaven, and will forgive their sin, and will heal their land." - II Chronicles 7:14

"And be not conformed to this world: but be ye transformed by the renewing of your mind, that ye may prove what is that good, and acceptable, and perfect, will of God."
- Romans 12:2

I grew up in the Syracuse, New York area. My Mom and Dad were always so good to us. I have two brothers and two sisters. We always did things together as a family. No matter what happened, Mom and Dad were always there. Even when Dad would get laid off sometimes from work, we always had food to eat and clothes on our backs.

My Dad worked two jobs many times to provide for our family. Growing up, my brothers and I all had the same paper route for twelve years, four years each. Mom and Dad always taught us to have a good work ethic. My Mom was one of the best cooks that I knew. I really miss that now. She would always make hats and mittens for us to wear in the wintertime. My Mom reminds me of the woman spoken of in Proverbs Chapter 31 that provides for her family.

I grew up going to a Methodist church — at one time, the Methodists preached salvation. My Mom was saved in the Methodist church when they preached salvation. I never learned how to be saved at the Methodist Church; it was never discussed when I attended. My parents left the Methodist Church when things were not being done the way they should be. Somebody invited us to go to Buckley Road Baptist Church, which changed our whole family. We attended church on Sunday mornings, Sunday nights, and even started going on Wednesday nights. They taught the Bible there, and I learned that you needed to be saved to go to Heaven. I was around twelve or thirteen years old, and one Sunday morning, I went forward to be saved. Norm Gore showed me from the Bible how to be saved. I thank the Lord for this day in my life. My Mom and Dad, after a while, even bought a bus to start a bus ministry.

When I was fifteen years old, we moved to South Bend, Indiana, for my Dad to get a job. Jobs in the Syracuse, New York area in the early '70s were scarce. My Dad, who worked at GE, got laid off, along with over 20,000 people. Before we moved, I was even able to help start building a new church building. When we moved to South Bend, we went to a large Baptist church. There were around one hundred teens in our youth group. There were excellent pastors in this church. They had a massive bus ministry with over ten buses. My Mom and Dad ran one of the bus routes. They also had a large Christian school where my Mom worked as a teacher. When Pastor Kennedy left, another pastor came. The church started going downhill from there. This is what happens when pastors are not doing what God wants them to do. I was always active in church, but not always in the way I should have been. When I graduated from high school, I started a lawn care and landscaping business. I took a landscaping correspondence course and am grateful to some landscaping professionals who assisted me in learning how to handle everything. I had men from my church working for me. I even had pastors over the years to work for me.

After a neighbor complained about my landscaping business on our property, and I could not find a property to relocate to, I moved back to New York, where I worked for a landscape company.

I was the foreman in our crew. When my Dad retired, he and my Mom moved back to New York. I built a small greenhouse to grow nursery stocks. Dad wanted to grow some flowers, so I ordered some geraniums for him. Dad and Mom both loved growing plants. Mom and Dad loved this property in Fulton, New York; it had twenty-one acres. One day, when I was working for the landscaping company, I was called off the job and was told I needed to go home. My Dad had a heart attack while driving and went off the road right around the corner from our house, and died. This was something that we never would expect to happen; he was only 65 years old. Dad was always out working in the yard or field planting trees for me. We never know when the Lord is going to call us home.

> *"Therefore, be ye also ready: for in*
> *such an hour as ye think not the*
> *son man cometh." - Matthew 24:44*

After this, it was just Mom and me, so I built another greenhouse because she enjoyed growing plants. I looked at getting into running heavy equipment with the union hall, a job I would have loved doing. I found out that if I had gotten the position, I would have to travel wherever the work was. I did not want to leave my Mom alone all the time.

Mom and Dad had done so much for me; I felt I needed to take care of my Mom. I quit the landscaping job after three years because they were not paying me for using my equipment. I started my own landscaping business again. I was doing landscape business and greenhouse business. We had about a ½ acre of greenhouses. I was going to church but not serving the Lord the way I should. Even though I had taught Sunday school and did a lot of door-to-door knocking and passing out tracts, my heart was not always in it.

In the mid-'90s, I opened up a garden center but had a lot of struggles with this. In all honesty, I believe this was not the Lord's will for me, and it was what I wanted. I ran this garden center for the last two years after firing my manager along with the farm. To this day, I still do not want to know everything that went on at the garden center; I had heard and seen enough. This garden center was twenty miles from our farm, where we grew everything. It took many hours to deal with both properties, along with having employees at both places. I did not like leaving mom alone at the farm all the time, so I sold the garden center. We never had our garden center open on Sundays. We had employees who wanted to open it up on Mother's Day. I told them I would not do this because the Lord would not bless it. I thank the Lord for watching over me for all the hours I worked there. I know this; I tried to be a good testimony there and always had tracts on my counter. All the policemen in that area knew my schedule, how I would come and water the plants on Sundays after going to church. After selling that garden center, we started one at the farm. We already had a deposit on a new greenhouse that was supposed to go up at our other garden center, so we put it up at the farm. Mom helped in running this garden center for me. She would wait on customers, and she had gotten to know many of them. She did this, although she would have rather stayed working in the greenhouse. I thank the Lord for everything I could do for the different churches that I have been in over the years. I did landscaping, brickwork, backhoe work, and even assisted with the construction of a brand-new church structure.

When we try to do things our way and they don't work, the Lord doesn't bless us. As Christians, we need to be out and about telling God's simple plan of salvation. I am sorry I wasted so many years because I could have been a better testimony for the Lord. As Christians, we need to be living what God teaches from His Word. I know this is not always popular today, but when we live for Jesus Christ, others can see the difference in our lives which can encourage others to put their lives in God's hands. God has a gift for everyone willing to accept it. This gift is eternal salvation in Heaven with the Lord. People are dying and going to Hell every single day.

I have had many people say, "Why would a loving God allow people to go to Hell?" People do not go to hell for their sins. They go to Hell for the one sin of rejecting Jesus Christ, the One who died for them. God cannot allow any sin into Heaven; it is a pure and clean place. We all have a choice to make, whether we want to accept the Lord or not.

All of us have sinned, and unless we receive the Lord to come into our hearts and lives, we will not get into Heaven. We can do all the things we want for God; giving money, working in the church, etc., but without knowing Him personally, we will not get into Heaven.

> *"For the wages of sin is death; but*
> *the gift of God is eternal life*
> *through Jesus Christ our Lord."*
> *-Romans 6:23*

Mom loved working in the greenhouses, which I believe is what kept her alive for so long after Dad had passed away. She was one of my best employees. Over the years, we grew a wide variety of plants and sold them wholesale to other garden centers and at farmers' markets. We even started growing hydroponic vegetables. Around three in the afternoon, one early spring day in 2012, I came up to get the laundry off the line for Mom; I had no idea that it would be the last time I would be able to speak to her. I called Mom on our two-way radio around 5 p.m., and she did not answer.

Sometimes Mom would put the 2-way radio down, so I did not think anything about it. I waited until 6 p.m., and she still did not answer, so I went to the house to see what was wrong. I found her in her bathroom gasping for breath; she had a severe stroke. To this day, I can still remember the condition I found her in. We took her to the hospital, and we ended up removing life support off because there was too much damage to the brain. That was the hardest week of my life, watching Mom die. We never know why God allows things like this to happen to us, but I know God always has a reason and a purpose for it. Some nights when I drove home from the hospital, I didn't even remember some of the roads I was on until I had gotten home. I had taken care of my Mom for over twenty years after Dad had passed away. I thank the Lord for being able to be there to take care of my Mom. She went through many health issues but never gave up on the Lord. She had breast cancer, went through two pacemakers, and had her hip replaced twice. One thing I will tell anyone who still has their parents is to thank them for everything they've done. I did not thank my parents enough. When I get to Heaven, the first thing I will do is thank my Mom and Dad.

After Mom's death, I got very discouraged and let things go with my business. I was not putting all my faith in God as I should have. We always need to be ready to meet the Lord; we never know when He may call us home to be with Him.

"Watch therefore: for ye know not what hour your Lord doth come."
- Matthew 24:42

There were many days when I thought of ending my life. I know this is not what the Lord wants us to do. I decided to try attending another church out in the country, which was one of the best things I had done in my life. Pastor Lagoe and Pastor Kinney were a real encouragement to me. The messages there helped me draw closer to the Lord than I had been in a long time. Emmanuel Bible Baptist Church was out in the country, but it was larger than some nearby cities. This church is still growing because Pastor Lagoe has a burden for souls. This church also has many outreach ministries with people willing to serve the Lord. There is no reason I should even be alive because I fell asleep driving so many times, even when driving a truck doing deliveries. The Lord had His hand on the steering wheel so many times for me. I know the Lord has a purpose for me to still be alive.

"Speaking to yourselves in psalms and hymns and spiritual songs, singing and making melody in your heart to the Lord; giving thanks always for all things unto God and the Father in the name of our Lord Jesus Christ."

- Ephesians 5:19-20

After the growing season of 2015, I decided to close the garden center because we did not have enough sales. I was doing our hydroponics and selling it to stores and schools. We went through a long process to get our business certified with the U.S. government for our hydroponics. I tried to sell my business in the spring of 2016, and thought a young man would buy it and was offered a job in Virginia. I moved to Virginia and worked there.

I left my greenhouse business in the hands of one of my employees to run it for me. I did all the bookkeeping while I was working at my current job. It was a beautiful place to live in the Blue Ridge Mountains, and I found a good church. I worked at a large greenhouse operation. This was a relatively easy job for me compared to what I had done in the past. The sale of my property fell through, and I ended up moving back to New York. I was working at the greenhouses growing hydroponic lettuce but did not have enough sales to keep it going. I started selling off equipment and greenhouses to pay the bills.

I even closed the greenhouses down for a while and worked for another greenhouse operation. This greenhouse operation was a sizeable hydroponic grower that was over an hour drive from my house each way. Several people approached me about starting the greenhouses back up and growing hydroponic vegetables again. They worked with the state and were able to get us grant money to start back up. We were growing for a food hub in Watertown, New York. The man in charge of this food hub was not easy to work with. Most of our products were going to the schools in that area. The man didn't pay bills on time and wouldn't buy all the products we grew for him. We donated and gave a lot of products to different food banks.

In March of 2018, I got very discouraged by the way things were going. I was not paying attention to what the Lord wanted me to do and decided to end my life. This should never have happened if I had been putting my faith and trust in the Lord. It was a very snowy day, and I decided to walk through the woods and jump in the creek behind my house. I sat there for quite a while but could not do it. I went back home and called Pastor Lagoe, but he did not answer his phone. I left a message saying that I wanted to end my life. I found out later on; he had been up all night with a family that had lost a baby. I decided to go and try jumping in the creek again.

I did not do it and lay in the snow instead for a very long time until the State Police found me. Many state troopers were involved in this operation, along with two ambulance crews and firefighters, to get me out of the woods. I ruined my testimony by doing this. I knew one of the state troopers, and his father owned a greenhouse operation. I am sure that the word had gotten around about what I had done. All the people in the area knew that I was a Christian. I sent a thank you card to the state troopers and ambulance crew for rescuing me, along with an apology for what I had done.

After being in the hospital in Syracuse under 24-hour observation, they moved me to a mental ward in Rome, New York. Pastor Lagoe was very angry with me for doing this, and he had the right to be. While in the mental ward, the Lord brought me to my senses, and I asked the Lord to forgive me for what I had done. I was able to give my testimony to all the nurses and doctors there. I spent most of my time in my room reading the Bible. I was released after only three days there. This was the Lord's will because the doctor said that it was not normal. Nobody in their right mind would want to be in a place like that. The Lord has been so good to me even when I have made so many mistakes.

"Brethren, I count not myself to have apprehended: but this one thing I do, forgetting those things which are behind and reaching forth unto those things which are before."
- Philippians 3:13

In April of 2018, the business was not making enough money to keep things going. The Lord was still supplying my needs as He always did for me. I decided to put the business up for sale again. This time I told the Lord I would go where He wanted me to go and do what He wanted me to do. I put everything I had in the Lord's hands and wanted His leading and direction in my life. I started looking for a job closer to my sister and brother in the Midwest. I had two companies that wanted to interview me. One was in Indiana, and the other was in Minnesota. I traveled to both of these operations to talk to them and see their processes. I discussed these offers over with Pastor Lagoe and prayed to the Lord about which direction to take. I decided to take the job in Indiana; which was for a garden center manager position. I moved to Indiana and left my business in the hands of one of my employees again. When I went to this job for the interview, they had all kinds of crafts and signage around their shop talking about God. I thought they might be Christians but found out very fast after working for them a short while they were not Christians, but they did go to church.

I had one of the employees tell me he would never go to the owner's church. They blamed all their problems on their managers, claiming that this was the reason the business was not doing well.

While working for them, I was still taking care of all the finances and business issues in New York. The Lord will judge all of us for what we do and how we act. I worked very hard for them and many hours there, even on Sunday afternoons, when it was supposed to be my day off.

The reason the Lord may have sent me to this job was to serve as a testimony to the employees.

When leaving work one day, one of the employees and I gotten into a discussion about the Lord. I was able to share my testimony with her. This was an encouragement to her, and I thanked the Lord for this. She had been very bitter at the Lord for a divorce she had gone through. Sometimes we get resentful at the Lord when it is not His fault. In reality, it is our fault for not paying attention to what He wants us to be doing all of the time.

On September 1, 2018, one of the employees and I loaded a large tree on a customer's truck. We were the only employees there that day. I did not know I had hurt my back until two days later. I had X-rays done and had several issues going on. I was told I should not be picking up anything heavy. I went back to work after several days off. One day, my left leg went completely numb. I talked to the owners about my health situation, and they said they would help with doctor bills and take it out of my pay because I had no insurance. I knew this was not something I should do with them, the way they ran their business. Then one morning, the owner's wife said she had a waiver she wanted me to sign. She put it on my desk and left. I waited all day for her to come back. She had not returned by 4 p.m., and I was in a lot of pain. The waiver said they would not be responsible for me on the property; I refused to sign it and decided it was better to quit than be fired. I turned in all my keys and left. Having been an owner myself for many years, I know this is not how you treat your employees. Now I am out of work, had no insurance, and had health problems. I have often found out that when we put our faith and trust in God, He will supply our needs.

"But my God shall supply all your needs according to his riches in glory by Christ Jesus." - Philippians 4:19

Not only did I have pain in my back and leg, but I also ended up with shingles. The Lord allowed me to get insurance and some treatment with doctors. He supplied my needs each week with finances I had not expected. I had accepted an offer on my property in New York at the end of August, but things were going very slowly. This meant paying all the bills from my business plus rent on the apartment that I lived in. I could not even go back to New York and move the rest of my belongings with my health issues. My brother-in-law and nephew went back in October, and with the help of friends back there, packed everything up and moved it to Indiana. After going to physical therapy for eight weeks, my pain was finally almost gone. I figured I would have to live with a numb leg, but that was okay if it was what the Lord wanted. The numbness lasted for three months before it finally went away. The owners where I had worked lied to the workers about my back issues, and I was denied any compensation. They are the ones who will have to live with what they have done. The Lord has been so good to me with everything He has done. I am waiting on Him for what He wants me to do next. I know He has a plan for me; otherwise, I would not still be alive. Finally, my house in New York closed in December. I wasn't happy with who bought it, but I did not have many options. Two women had bought it and planned to grow hemp in the greenhouses.

With all my health issues, I was not sure if I would be able to work again. I began looking online for a job. A company wanted to hire me. This job entailed purchasing and shipping products for them in the United States. I looked into every aspect of this business. I had the managers' names, addresses, phone numbers, and federal identification numbers. I thought I had enough information on them to be a legal company. After working for them for a short while, it just did not seem right what I was doing. When I started this job, they paid off my charge cards. I was to buy the products for them on my charge cards, then they would pay me back. I told my manager that I did not want to do this job anymore because I felt this was the Lord wanted me to do. She told me to buy one more iPad, and then she would end the contract. After buying and shipping this last iPad, it brought me even with what they had paid off on my charge cards. I figured I was all done with this company.

After selling my property in New York, I paid all my charge cards and bills. I was debt-free for the first time in many years. Two weeks later, when I received my charge card bill, the company I had worked for reversed their payment. I had just lost over $21,000. To this day, I have not been able to get it resolved. I have worked with the state and the federal government. It costs me $350 every month for five years to pay this debt off. Even with this, the Lord is still providing for my needs.

"And all things, whatsoever ye shall ask in prayer, believing, ye shall receive."
- Matthew 21:22

I hired an attorney to help with my workers' compensation case in December 2018. This was a prolonged process of working through all the paperwork. In July of 2019, I had to appear in front of a court-appointed person who documented what happened. I was interrogated for two hours by the attorney from the company where I had worked. She went back to the beginning of my career, forty years ago. Through all of this, I gave my testimony of what God had done for me. This was done in front of my lawyer, their lawyer, and the business owners of the company where I had worked. I thank the Lord for giving me the boldness to do this. It has taken over a year to resolve this situation.

In March of 2020, I received a check for the settlement. My attorney wanted to try to get more money, but I felt the Lord wanted me to resolve this situation. It was not a large check, but I know the Lord will make this money go a long way. The Lord always works things out when we put our faith and trust in Him.

> *"And we know all things work*
> *together for good to them that love*
> *God, to them who are called*
> *according to his purpose."*
> *- Romans 8:28*

In the spring of 2019, I worked for a greenhouse use operation. This job really wore on me doing all the carrying, loading, and unloading of trucks. By June, I was worn out and did not work for the last couple of days. My whole body was hurting by the time I had finished.

While working for the greenhouse operation, I was able to find a house. I bought this house that needed a lot of work, but it was cheaper than paying rent on my apartment and storage unit. The Lord worked this whole thing out to be able to buy this house. It was only two weeks after the closing of my house that I was done working at the greenhouse operation. I sold my delivery van from my past business to get the roof, gutters, and windows replaced. I kept applying for jobs that were not so labor-intensive, but nobody would hire me. I remodeled the house I bought because it had been vacant for two years.

I had a lot of issues doing it because I could work only a couple of hours at a time and was worn out. I'm not sure what is going on with my health, but I'm just leaving it in the Lord's hands. The inability to work like I used to really frustrates me. When you are 60 years old and have a terrible back, nobody wants to hire you.

I decided in the fall to start doing custom wood signs. I have always liked working with wood. I went to several craft shows trying to sell the signs but did not sell many. I have been putting all my faith and trust in God to supply my needs. I had a magnificent vegetable garden which helped out with my food bill and was able to can and freeze a lot for the winter.

"I can do all things through Christ
which strengtheneth me." - Philippians 4:13

We see many things going on around us every single day that do not please the Lord. Then we hear about all kinds of shootings, killings, and terrible things that happen to people. A lot of this comes from all the violent video games and movies made today, plus all the trash on the internet. We see the various storms, fires, diseases, and earthquakes that take many lives and damage many properties. I know the Lord does not cause all of these, but He allows them for a purpose.

I believe He is trying to wake people up to the fact that He is still in control. When these storms come, Christians need to be ready to help people physically and, more importantly, spiritually. The Lord is only going to give us so much time before He returns to this earth.

"Therefore, be ye also ready: for in such an hour as ye think not the Son of man cometh."
- Matthew 24:44

I applied for disability in the fall of 2019 because I had not been able to get a job and was not selling much with my sign business. I kept putting this off because it was not what I wanted to do. I was praying to the Lord about how He would meet my needs, and I wasn't sure if this was going to be one of them. It's a lengthy procedure with a lot of paperwork. The first time I applied for disability, they turned me down. I have gone back to them for reconsideration; I'm not sure whether this will go through this time or not. It is all in the Lord's hands.

In February of 2020, while working in my woodshop, I caught my hand in the wood planer and had to go to the hospital and have three fingers put back together. I was very thankful that the doctors were able to save my fingers.

I do not know all the reasons why these things happen, but God must have a plan. One day, very early in the morning in March 2020, I heard a still small voice from the Lord on what to do. The Lord gave me the idea of making lawn furniture. I used to sell lawn furniture in my garden center. After receiving my worker's compensation check and taking some money out of my life insurance, I could catch up on paying my bills off. I talked to the greenhouse owners where I worked in the spring of 2019 about putting my furniture there. They said we could work that out. They wanted me to come back to work for them. I told them I could not right now with my fingers still healing and my heart issue. I have started working on building some lawn chairs to sell. I am not sure if I will sell much right now with the coronavirus going around. Thank the Lord for my fingers healing and that I can work with them again. I was able to sell several chairs and tables throughout the summertime. I also was able to sell several planters from free wood. The Lord is so faithful to us when we put our trust in Him.

"Know therefore that the Lord thy God, He is God, the faithful God, which keepeth covenant and mercy with them that love Him and keep his commandments to a thousand generations;" - Deuteronomy 7:9

After going through many different tests for my heart and wearing a heart monitor for two weeks, the doctors decided to put a pacemaker in me.

My heart was up and down so much they felt that they could control it with a pacemaker and medicine. I am praying that this will allow me to feel better and do more work. The Lord always knows what is best for us, even when we do not. I had to put off having my heart checked for some time. After having the pacemaker put in, it did not seem to help with my health too much. The doctors wanted to do more tests. They decided to do a heart catheterization on me and did not find anything wrong. I will not go through any more tests; I am just going to live with whatever is going on. I am not sure what the Lord's plan is for me, but He must still have work for me to do because I'm still here. I am ready to go home to be with the Lord at any time, whether He calls me home or returns for me.

I started getting dizzy spells while driving in October and went to the doctor to see what was happening. I went numerous times and had different tests done. The doctor was not sure what was causing it. They sent me to an ear, nose, and throat doctor. I had quite a bit of wax in one of my ears; it took a while, but I finally got it cleaned out. Then the doctor did all kinds of ear tests. After getting my ear cleaned out, it helped a lot. I was still not able to drive at night; it bothers my eyes too much.

For the second time, disability denied offering me any help. I've decided to let my attorney deal with it. I'm not sure whether this is the Lord's will or not for me to get disability; we will have to wait and see. I have not been able to get much in sales this winter either. All my funds are running out again, but I know we should not worry because God is in control. He will always supply our needs when we put our faith and trust in Him. This is something I always have to remember. I have been looking for a job that I might be able to do. With several health issues going on, I have not been able to find anything. I started to write some poems this winter.

In the spring of 2021, I started working with Home Advisors to get woodworking jobs. I have refinished tables and chairs, and fixed tables and chairs. I even built a new coffee table for one lady. In the summer, I even made kitchen cabinets and installed them. It has been working out pretty well in helping with my finances. In July, I started to receive my Social Security. I dropped my disability case because this is what I thought the Lord wanted me to do. Even though I have had some health issues, the Lord has been so good to me.

Who Cares for the Birds

How the birds fly so free, how the birds sail with ease through the air. They glide as free as can be, with no care. They have nothing to worry about because the Lord is always there. When we look at the birds who are always cared for by one so tender and fair. Why should we worry or fear, God is always there?

Lily of the Valley

The lily of the valley, so pretty and fair. How it grows without care. God has created each and every one of these. So beautiful and fair, they will lighten our cares. When we put our faith and trust in God, He cares for us, just as He will for the lily. So, look to the Lord to brighten your days so your light will shine to others always.

How the Garden Grows

How the garden grows when it is taken care of with tender love and care. The seeds are sown in good ground and spring up everywhere. When God provides the sun and the rain, the seeds will grow and flourish into beautiful, heavenly flowers everywhere.

God's Trees

The trees in the springtime are so pretty and fair, with all their beauty and fragrance that fill the air. In summertime, the trees provide shade so cool and fair that everyone wants to be there. In the fall, the trees are so pretty with all their colors bright and clear, that you can see them everywhere. In the winter, the trees stand out with all the snow glistening on them so pure and clean, we know that this can only happen with God's tender love and care.

In the first part of April, I was diagnosed with another hernia. Before this surgery could be done it had to be approved with my heart doctor. They set it up for surgery at the end of April. Went to the cardiologist for a check-up, and while there, I mention having shortness of breath. That was all it took and they canceled my surgery.

The doctors wanted to do more test on me and decided to do a stress test on me. They knew that I could not do the tread mill so they decided on the nuclear test.

On May 2nd, 2024, I drove myself to have a stress test at the hospital. My cardiologist wanted this done because of shortness of breath. That morning, I was feeling better than I was in several days. That all changed in a very short time. Within 3 hours, I was admitted to the emergency room with shortness of breath and dizziness; everything was spinning. They ran all kinds of tests on me. The cardiologist came and told me that I had failed the second half of the stress test, but thought I could go home. The nurse in charge of the emergency room that day thought I could go home also. I told her that I could not drive, I was still too dizzy, would have to call for a ride. She sent in another nurse that tried to get me up out of bed. When getting me up she said do not fall, I said I did not plan on that, we got as far as the door of the room and she said you are not going anywhere, back in bed. They admitted me into the hospital and did more tests. The next morning, they said they were going to do a heart cath. When they did the heart cath they did find a blockage, but did not put any stents in it. Said if they put any stents in, I could not have the hernia surgery for six months, they knew that I needed before that. They took me to intensive care for recovery from the heart cath. I asked the nurse if I would be able to drive home.

She thought I could and held me as long as she could. Around 5:30, the nurse let me go to the bathroom and get dressed. When I was on the toilet and looked down, where they had done the heart cath, it started to bleed all over. Hurried up and put my hand over the sink and pulled the emergency cord with my other hand. Two nurse's aides came in and wrapped it up with a towel. Once they got it stopped the nurse put the tourniquet back on as tight as she could, which turned my whole hand purple. They ordered dinner for me and kept me till the end of her shift, which was 7 p.m. The nurse then let me drive home. If this would have happened a half hour later than it did, when I was driving home it could have been a totally different story. I knew that the Lord still had a plan for me to be here.

"For the Lord thy God will hold thy right hand, saying unto thee, Fear not; I will help thee." - Isaiah 41:13

"I the Lord have called thee in righteousness, and will hold thine hand, and will keep thee," - Isaiah 42:6

I believe that the Lord wants me to somehow to be getting my testimony out to other churches and people what the Lord can do for them when we put our faith and trust in God. I have been able already to share this with number of nurses and people about what the Lord did for me in this situation. I was praying about the need for a new printer and the Lord opened the door much quicker than I expected for the finances to get it. I was able to get some of my books and Jesus bridges into the hospital for people to pick up. The Lord allowed the right person there when I needed it. He is so good to me all the time.

There are so many churches that I would call dead churches today in America. There is no growth in them, no people being saved or baptized. This needs to change I believe if we ever want to see the Lord bless America again.

"The Lord is my light and my salvation; whom shall I fear? The Lord is the strength of my life; of whom shall I be afraid? - Psalm 27:1

We are not to be afraid of people who do not love God. He will always watch over us.

"But the salvation of the righteous is of the Lord: he is their strength in the time of trouble." -Psalm 37:39

We do not have to be afraid of what is going on around us because the Lord is our strength and rock. We are commanded by God to be serving Him for those of us that are Christians. This includes reading our Bible every day and spending time in prayer with our Lord. God has brought me closer to

Him than I have ever been. I cannot thank the Lord enough for all that He has done for me. How He supplies my needs all the time even when I do not have any wood working. My bills are always paid on time. We serve such a wonderful God. I do not know how anyone today can get by without the Lord on their side. It is time as Christians we wake up and see the need to be letting our light shine for God. The same thing for the churches, they need to get on fire for the Lord. There are a lot of people out there that are hurting and need help, as Christians that is what we are supposed to be doing.

"Preach the word; be instant in season, out of season; reprove, rebuke, exhort with all long suffering and doctrine. For the time will come when they will not endure sound doctrine; but after their own lust shall they heap to themselves teachers, having itching ears; and they shall turn away their ears from the truth, and shall be turned unto fables." - II Timothy 4:2-4

This definitely is happening now. On May 21, 2024 I had to go in for the hernia surgery. Well, there I was able again to share my testimony to the nurses and how the Lord still must have a purpose for me being here. The Lord watches over us all the time, even when going into surgery we do not have to be afraid. Just put all your faith and trust in God.

Everything went fine with this operation, just a lot of pain, this is the second time having this done.

In August, one night, I was in church on a Wednesday night and started having pains in my chest while the pastor was preaching. Sometimes I get pains where my pacemaker is, and they do not last too long, this pain just kept getting worse and I did not want interrupt the service. Waited till the service was over, then told them I was having chest pains. They called the ambulance, and they took me to the emergency room. When the doctor came in to talk to me, he asked what the pastor was preaching on. After going through more test, they decided to keep me overnight. The next day, they decided to do another heart cath on me since they knew I had a blockage. They got me all prepped to do the heart cath, and had an emergency and had to take me back to my room. After a while, they came back for me, performed the heart cath, and placed a stent. Kept me over night. I am so thankful for the insurance taking care of this. Just to have the one stent put in was $70,000. Through all this, I was able to share my testimony numerous of times with doctors and nurses. The Lord has shown me again how He has been there for me so many years.

Some of us have physical heart issues, but we all have spiritual heart issues that surface in different ways. These include bitterness, jealousy, unforgiveness, and unthankfulness. Singing and praying from the heart can help us to overcome these things. As one of the songs we sing sometimes is "Count Your Many Blessings". If we would do this more often what a difference this could make in our lives. We all have so many things to be thankful for. I know I could go on for quite a while on all the things that I am thankful for.

"Speaking to yourselves in psalms and hymns and spiritual songs, singing and making melody in your heart to the Lord: Giving thanks always for all things unto God and the father in the name of our Lord Jesus Christ." - Ephesian 5: 19-20

Proverbs was written by Solomon the wise of men. When we read a proverb every day it can be such a help to us. When I read them, I look at them as going down the straight and narrow path or the wide and broad path. The Lord shows how we can get wisdom, knowledge, understanding and instructions which we need to stay on that straight and narrow path. We all need these in our life.

"Enter in ye in at the strait gate: for wide is the gate, and broad is the way, that leadeth to destruction, and many there be which go in thereat; Because strait is the gate, and narrow is the way, which leadeth unto life, and few there be that find it."
- Matthew 7:13-14

Since Proverbs has 31 chapters in it you can read one every day. This has been such a help to me since I have been doing this, it gives the encouragement and strength we need each day. I am writing this so it could be help to others. The Lord will help us all when we pay attention to what the Lord wants us to be doing. We can see in reading the proverbs how free will has such a part in staying on the straight and narrow path, free will normally will leads us down the wide path. Our free will is what causes most of us problems in our life. WE think God causes the problems in our life, but it is not God. He allows the things to happen that we have gotten ourselves into. When we are not serving the Lord the way we should, that's where we get into trouble. Many times, the way we want to do things is our own free will. We can see in the Bible many people that had gotten into trouble. Through all of these situations it was their own free will that put them where they ended up. Jonah, David, Joseph's brothers and many others. When we ask the Lord for His help and what difference that can make in our life.

"Ask, and it shall be given you; seek, and ye shall find; knock, and it shall be opened unto you: For everyone that asketh receiveth: and he that seeketh findeth; and to him that knocketh it shall be opened."
- Matthew 7:7-8

The Lord will never leave us or forsake us; He has given us that promise in His word the Bible.

I think about myself when I had gotten done with high school and wanted to lawn care and landscaping. I never asked the Lord if this is what He wanted me to be doing. What a difference this could have made in my life doing the Lord's will instead of my will. I want this book to be a help to young people about serving the Lord. There are so many things today that kids can get involved in this world that can ruin their life. I pray parents would be more involved with their kids in what they should be doing. Do not let them have a cell phone all the time. This is a big mistake with all the junk out there today. When we think about what we are doing is this our will or the Lords will.

I want to include an outline on a sermon that could help a lot of people today. All of us will go through storms in our life for one reason or another, the Lord told us we would. Many times, these storms can draw us closer to the Lord.

Discerning the storm.

For this you will want to read Luke 12:54, I Kings 19:11-12 and Jonah 1

1. <u>**What causes the storm**</u>

Going in the wrong direction. We can see what Jonah was doing, running from the Lord. Then he went to sleep, not paying attention to what was going on. How often do we do this in our own life. When the Lord is shown us what He wants us to be doing and we decide that we do not want to go that direction. We instead try to do it on our own, and it never works. I know this to be true in my own life. When I had my greenhouse business I put many hours into it for my own and not for the Lord. We stir up the storm when doing it on our own. This is disobedience to the Lord. When we cause a storm, it can cost others around us. Think about our families what cost is it to them, just like we see with Jonah and the other men in the boat. I know should have spent more time with my mom than I did. We need to be responsible for what we do. Go to the Lord and ask forgiveness for what we have done.

2. <u>Stilling the storm</u>

For this you will want to read Luke 8:22-25, Matthew 8:23-27, Mark 4:35-41, II Timothy 1:7 and Psalms 107:21-31

When reading all the passages we see how the disciples became fearful. Fear takes away sound thinking. We let the circumstances get in the way. How often do we let the circumstances in our own lives get in the way of serving the Lord and going in the right direction.

We get fearful when we are not putting our trust in the Lord and doing what He wants us to be doing. We need to build our solid rock upon the Lord Jesus Christ. When fear comes stop and wait upon the Lord. He will show us what to do. Do not make any decisions when in the storm. God will always get us to the other side. Just keep our trust in the Lord. When the Lord is knocking at our door, open it and let Him in. Wait and see the marvelous work He can do for you. I know in my life how many times I would have been better off to have waited upon the Lord than doing it my way. Time and time again He has gotten me through the storms of my life which most of them I caused. When you have your own business and employees it can cause many storms to rise up, when not paying attention to what you should be doing.

3. Standing in the storm

You will want to read for this Acts 27:14-25, Ephesians 4:1-7 and 4:22, and II Timothy 1:8-9

Our life is not our own when we are saved. We belong to God. We are to walk worthy of the vocation wherewith we are called. We are not to be ashamed of the testimony of our Lord. God gives us grace. When others are going through a storm, we as Christians are to be able to help them through. We are able to tell others of the storms that God has gotten us through, thereby being a help to them.

When I hurt my back and could not work for two years, the Lord always supplied my needs. When storms seem dark around us, we need to be on our face before the Lord in prayer. Be waiting on God what His plans are and be continually in His word. When reading His word, always pray before you start and ask the Lord for guidance. We need to be a witness in the storm to others and not let it get us down. Brag on the Lord what He can do for you by putting your faith and trust in Him.

After reading my testimony, I pray that it has been a help and encouragement to you. If you do not know where you will spend eternity after reading this, please read the verses at the end. These verses are from the Bible, and they will show you how you can be saved and show you where you are going to spend eternity. When you die, there are only two places that you will go, either to heaven or hell. This is plainly shown in the Bible. There is no in-between or anything else. I want to thank the Lord for His help and encouragement in writing this short story of my life.

"Trust in the Lord with all thine heart: and lean not unto thine own understanding. In all thy ways acknowledge him, and he shall direct thy paths."
- Proverbs 3:5-6

Romans Road Map to Heaven

1. "As it is written, there is none righteous, no not one." - Romans 3:10
2. "For all have sinned, and come short of the glory of God;" - Romans 3:23
3. "But God commandeth his love toward us, in that while we were yet sinners, Christ died for us." - Romans 5:8
4. "Wherefore, as by one man sin entered into the world, and death by sin; and so, death passed upon all men, for that all have sinned;" - Romans 5:12
5. "For the wages of sin is death; but the gift of God is eternal life through Jesus Christ our Lord." - Romans 6:23
6. "That if thou shalt confess with thy mouth the Lord Jesus, and shalt believe in thine heart that God hath raised from the dead, thou shalt be saved. For with the heart man believeth unto righteousness; and with the mouth confession is made unto salvation." - Romans 10:9-10
7. "For whosoever shall call upon the name of the Lord shall be saved." - Romans 10:13

For questions or help you may call me at 812-757-4148.

I pray this message may have been a help to you. Maybe you know someone going through a storm and would like to share this with them. I spend a lot of time in pray every day. If you have a prayer request and would like me to pray for you just let me know. You can reach me at my email *panurs130@att.net*. I felt it was time to update my book with the different things that have taken place in my life. The Lord is so good to us all the time, I can not stress that enough. If you know any youth groups or churches that would like me to share my testimony, please let me know, I would be glad to do it if possible. We should be looking up every day as we see the things happen around us in this world. Do not think we have much time left before the Lord returns.